ETF
TRADING
STRATEGIES
REVEALED

David Vomund,
Featuring: Linda Bradford Raschke,
Steve Palmquist, and Dr. J.D. Smith

Marketplace Books
Columbia, Maryland

This book, along with other books, is available at discounts that make it realistic to provide it as a gift to your customers, clients, and staff. For more information on these long lasting, cost effective premiums, please call us at (800) 272-2855 or you may email us at sales@traderslibrary.com.

ISBN 1-59280-258-3

Printed in the United States of America.

Contents

Introduction

This book presents a revolutionary approach to making money using classic technical analysis trading techniques. How can something be both revolutionary and classic? We apply classic technical analysis techniques to a new and growing investment vehicle—the Exchange-Traded Fund.

Many books claim to reveal revolutionary new trading techniques. Like fad diets, these techniques slowly fade away to be replaced with other "new and improved" systems. The approach in this book is different. We apply classic technical analysis techniques that have worked in the past and because of their simplicity will continue to work in the future.

The techniques and mechanical trading systems covered in the book are easy to learn and can be successfully employed by most people. That doesn't mean this material is bedtime reading. Using a highlighter and a notepad would be appropriate.

The book is divided into four parts.

Part I describes what ETFs are and how they work. It includes all that is needed to start succeeding in ETF investing.

Part II details the classic technical analysis technique of using chart analysis to trade ETFs. Both short-term and longer-term methods are discussed.

Part III covers simple but highly effective mechanical ETF rotation techniques. These techniques are applied to the different categories of ETFs (style, sector, and international) that are now available to the individual investor.

Part IV takes a brief look at trading psychology. While we offer several highly effective techniques, they work best when tailored to your personal trading style and when you have the emotional discipline to follow them. This is an important subject and is often ignored, to the detriment of many traders.

In creating this book, our goal was to include all the relevant material necessary for trading of ETFs, while leaving out the fluff. We attempted to incorporate in this book as much useful information as one would find in a book ten times its size. We believe our mission is accomplished. We think you'll agree.

ETF
TRADING
STRATEGIES
REVEALED

Part I

THE BASICS OF ETFs

Part I is a brief description of Exchange-Traded Funds and how they work—all you need to know to successfully trade them.

Exchange-Traded Funds (ETFs) are the fastest growing financial product in the United States. While still small, many expect they will eventually overtake mutual funds in assets. Mutual fund companies are aware of this and the largest fund families—Fidelity and Vanguard—have introduced their own ETFs.

If you desire more detailed information, check the web sites that we list near the end of the book. For a more comprehensive book on the subject, see Appendix I: Recommended Reading.

Chapter 1

First Things to Know about Exchange-Traded Funds

Exchange-Traded Funds (ETFs) have exploded in popularity. Outside of Wall Street, however, few people know what they are. That is changing. In time, ETFs will be as commonly known to people as mutual funds are.

ETFs were introduced in the United States in 1993 with the advent of the Standard & Poor's Depository Receipt, commonly known as S&P 500 Spyder (SPY). ETFs didn't become well known, however, until the late 1990s when the very popular Nasdaq 100 ETF (QQQQ) was introduced. Investors have quickly learned that ETFs provide a convenient way to gain market exposure to a domestic sector, a foreign market, or a commodity with one single transaction.

As a result, ETFs have become the fastest growing financial product in the United States. By the end of 2005, the number of publicly traded ETFs was about 200 with assets of around $300 billion.

ETFs are securities that combine elements of index funds, but do so with a twist. Like index funds, ETFs are pools of securities that track specific market indexes at a very low cost. Like stocks, ETFs are traded on major U.S. stock exchanges and can be bought and sold anytime during normal trading hours. Buy and sell orders are placed with any brokerage firm. Many of the execution tactics suitable for stocks can also be applied to ETFs, from stop and limit orders to margin buying. They can be shorted and often have options listed on them.

Diversification

Similar to index mutual funds, most ETFs represent ownership in an underlying portfolio of securities that tracks a specific market index. That index may cover an entire market, or slices of the market broken down by capitalization, sector, style, country, etc. So today's investor can buy an entire market segment, including international markets, with one trade.

ETFs track very closely to their underlying market index. Figure 1 shows the S&P Small-Cap 600 Value Index. Below that is the iShares S&P 600 Value ETF that tracks the above index. Notice that their price movement shows a nearly perfect correlation. That is to be expected. If they were to deviate, arbitrageurs would enter to profit from the discrepancy.

Owning a basket of securities is much more comfortable than owning a few individual stocks. With ETFs, you don't have to worry that your stock holding will gap down 20% after an unexpected profit warning is issued. Because of their diversification, the price movement in ETFs is more predictable than in individual stocks.

The strategies that will be outlined in this book are tactical in nature and are intended to strengthen a portfolio by diversifying it, yet channel the diversification toward specific, outperforming market sectors.

Costs

When it comes to running an investment fund, there will always be costs. These costs can include analyst fees, marketing costs, and

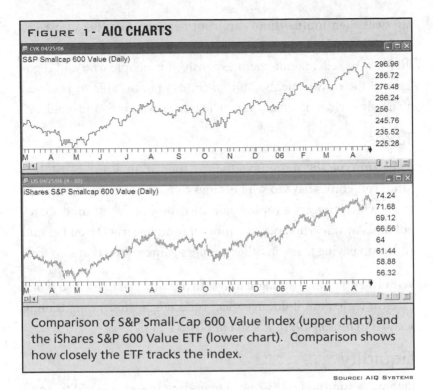

FIGURE 1 - AIQ CHARTS

S&P Smallcap 600 Value (Daily)

296.96
286.72
276.48
266.24
256
245.76
235.52
225.28

M   A   M   J   J   A   S   O   N   D   06   F   M   A

iShares S&P Smallcap 600 Value (Daily)

74.24
71.68
69.12
66.56
64
61.44
58.88
56.32

M   A   M   J   J   A   S   O   N   D   06   F   M   A

Comparison of S&P Small-Cap 600 Value Index (upper chart) and the iShares S&P 600 Value ETF (lower chart). Comparison shows how closely the ETF tracks the index.

SOURCE: AIQ SYSTEMS

administrative costs. Generally, index funds are cheaper to manage than actively managed funds. Since most ETFs are index funds, their expenses are generally well below those of actively managed mutual funds. Even when you compare similar products, ETF expenses are generally lower. For example, the Vanguard Index 500 has a very low expense ratio of 0.18% of assets, but the iShares S&P 500 ETF is cheaper still, with an expense ratio of 0.09%.

The biggest cost advantage of ETFs over traditional index mutual funds is in back-end expenses. Index mutual funds have to maintain the individual account balances and mail statements and must have a staff ready to open and close accounts. With ETFs, these expenses are eliminated, making funds cheaper to manage.

To be fair, there may be overriding reasons favoring mutual funds for some investors. For example, if you invest small sums at regular intervals then mutual funds are more appropriate. Because ETFs trade like stocks, investors pay a brokerage commission each time they buy or sell, making them expensive for people who add regularly to their investments. Mutual funds are also able to re-invest quarterly dividends, an advantage for those who buy-and-hold.

Taxes

ETFs are typically more tax efficient than mutual funds. Mutual funds sometimes have to sell holdings to meet the need of redemptions, which triggers a capital gain distribution for all fund shareholders. Anyone who bought a mutual fund in early December and ended up paying taxes on other people's gains knows that's no fun!

With ETFs, shares are bought and sold on the open market so if one investor cashes out it doesn't affect others. The after-hours trading scandal in mutual funds doesn't apply to ETFs.

Liquidity

Before assessing liquidity we need to understand what liquidity is and why the lack of it is a bad thing. A liquid investment is one that can quickly be bought and sold at its fair market value. Individual purchases and sales of the security should not affect its price. Liquidity is generally measured by the number of shares traded per day.

Thinly traded securities are considered illiquid. As a result, they have high spreads (the difference between the bid and the ask prices), which adversely affects the execution cost. Trading illiquid investments can be expensive.

Since ETFs trade like stocks, it's reasonable to assume their liquidity should be judged in the same manner as stocks. That's a common misconception about ETFs, even among Wall Street professionals.

Unlike stocks, the number of shares in an ETF is not fixed. That is, if the demand for a given ETF outstrips supply at any point, then a specialist may simply create new shares from a basket of the underlying securities in that fund. Shares are created or redeemed to meet demand. Therefore the liquidity of an ETF is not only defined by its volume, but also by the liquidity of its holdings. So you might see an international emerging market ETF with a lot of volume that is actually less liquid than a domestic large-cap value ETF that trades with lower volume.

If an ETF and a stock both have 30,000 shares traded on a particular day, the ETF will typically be more liquid. That is, your order is much less likely to move the price. In a few cases, block orders that I placed were more than half of the total volume for an ETF on a particular day. Expecting that it would take a long time to get a fair execution, I've been pleasantly surprised to get immediate execution at the market price.

For the typical investor, this should be comforting. It doesn't mean, however, that shares are created or redeemed for your order. This process is typically done for institutional investors that trade 50,000 shares or more. The party on the other side of most ETF transactions is a market maker or another investor. For most retail orders, a market order is sufficient. The bid-to-ask spreads in ETFs tend to be narrow and cover a large number of shares.

With that said, buying or selling ETFs with high daily volume is more attractive (in terms of spread) than trading ETFs with low volume. Unfortunately, many ETFs don't trade very much. Active traders should stick with the ETFs like the S&P 500 SPDR (SPY), Nasdaq 100 (QQQQ), or Russell 2000 (IWM), all of which have high volume and narrow spreads.

When you place an order for a low volume ETF, don't use a market order. Instead, place a limit order between the bid and the ask price. Unless it is a fast moving market, you'll almost always get a quick execution.

Part II

CHART ANALYSIS

P art II covers the important topic of chart interpretation. For help, I've turned to two technicians that I very much admire. Both are professional traders who strive for consistency—their goal is to make money in all market environments. At the core of their analysis is chart pattern interpretation. "The chart tells all."

Linda Bradford Raschke actively trades equities and futures. She explains how the same analysis techniques are successfully applied to trading ETFs. While the techniques may be the same, she explains how ETFs should be analyzed under different time horizons.

Steve Palmquist's contribution is a market adaptive approach. He varies his style of analysis based on the market condition. His article details his approach to trading, including buy, sell, and capitalization rules.

Chapter 2

Valuable Advice from Linda Bradford Raschke

L inda is president of LBRGroup, a CTA firm that manages money in both futures and equities. She is featured in Jack Schwager's book, *The New Market Wizards*, and co-authored the best selling book *Street Smarts—High Probability Short Term Trading Strategies*.

The following is an interview that I conducted with Linda focusing on methods for trading ETFs.

Linda Bradford Raschke

Vomund: Is it worth day-trading ETFs?

Raschke: In my opinion, no. There are far better vehicles for day-trading. Either futures or higher beta stocks are better. The problem is that few ETFs have the volume and liquidity for fast and effective execution, and the ones with sufficient volume tend to be the slower movers.

ETFs are so broad and encompassing that they can be classified into two groups. A small number of ETFs are heavily traded and very liquid, such as Spyder (SPY) that tracks the S&P 500, but most aren't liquid enough for active day-trading. Many global and sector ETFs might only trade 50,000 shares a day.

The vehicle you choose to use for day-trading depends on your execution platform, your commission structure, and your objectives. I know people who successfully trade the Spyder (SPY), but most professional day-traders will choose the E-mini S&P Futures instead because of the greater leverage.

The advantage of ETFs is that they cover such a broad spectrum. They allow investors to easily buy equities from many countries or individual sectors. And because an ETF contains a basket of stocks, one bad apple is usually offset by the other stock holdings. When you trade a basket of stocks, you'll do better trading a longer time frame as opposed to a shorter time frame. Longer time frame charts show smoother price movement and less noise.

Vomund: So professional day-traders typically aren't interested in trading ETFs. How about the trading investor? By that I mean someone who doesn't follow the market throughout the day but places trades with a holding period of several days to a few weeks.

Raschke: The more volatility and liquidity an individual market has, the shorter the time period that you can trade and use for your analysis. With ETFs, I'd use daily and weekly charts exclusively and turn off the real-time charts. If you placed an order on many of the foreign market ETFs, you might as well execute the order on the open or the close because these ETFs don't trade much throughout the day.

Still, whether you use intraday charts or weekly charts, you always go through the same process of determining if you should be a buyer or a seller, determining support and resistance, determining the trend, determining consolidation points, etc. The foreign ETFs were some of the best investment vehicles last year.

Vomund: What methods do you use to time your entry points?

Raschke: Because ETFs hold baskets of stocks and are more diversified than individual stocks, they respond very well to simple chart analysis. I believe that there are no more powerful tools than the techniques that have been written about in classic technical analysis literature. I trade the basic chart patterns like the triangle. I trade breakouts, and I trade pullbacks after breakouts.

This is simple stuff but it is all that is needed to be successful, and it eliminates a lot of the noise in the market when the techniques are applied correctly. Watch the previous swing highs and swing lows as well as the length of the swings up and down when timing entries.

Vomund: Can you give some examples?

Raschke: Sure. Because it has had lots of movement, let's look at the weekly chart of iShares Japan Fund (EWJ) (Figure 2). It is easy to

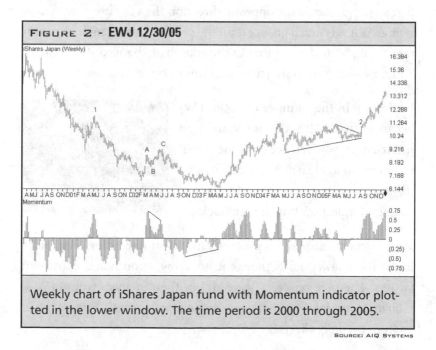

FIGURE 2 - **EWJ 12/30/05**

Weekly chart of iShares Japan fund with Momentum indicator plotted in the lower window. The time period is 2000 through 2005.

notice that during 2000-03 all the major swings were greater to the downside than the upside. Notice the lower highs and lower lows.

Within this time period there was a drop in 2001, followed by a reaction move to the upside (point 1). Since the trend is down, traders should short into this reaction. A second leg down ensued in 2001 followed by another reaction up. The reaction was also a classic ABC type move (rallies to point A, falls to a higher low in point B, and rallies above point A to point C) with a classical momentum divergence on the way up (see trendline on momentum indicator). This is one of the best shorting signals that you can get.

The last leg down had a clear loss of momentum, as the drop was not as great as the second leg lower. As a result, a positive divergence formed in the momentum indicator. That is, the oscillator made higher lows.

Then in June/July 2003 there was a very sharp spike up. This was the first swing greater in the opposite direction than the previous downswing. As it was much greater than the previous swing high, the summer swing high showed that the market had changed its character. You now switch from shorting reactions to buying pullbacks.

Beginning in the summer of 2004, EWJ began to drift. After the breakout from the triangle, you can see at point 2 that momentum made new highs confirming the breakout. An uptrend was in place so traders should now buy the pullbacks.

> Note:
> The momentum indicator is the difference between a 3-period and a 10-period simple moving average.

Weekly charts display longer-term moves and, as they filter out a lot of the market noise, they tend to show smooth and consistent swings. They are very easy to read, but their analysis will not provide many trades. More active traders can perform the same style of analysis on daily charts.

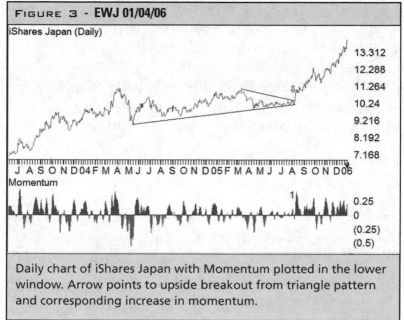

SOURCE: AIQ SYSTEMS

FIGURE 3 - EWJ 01/04/06

iShares Japan (Daily)

13.312
12.288
11.264
10.24
9.216
8.192
7.168

J A S O N D 04 F M A M J J A S O N D 05 F M A M J J A S O N D 06

Momentum

0.25
0
(0.25)
(0.5)

Daily chart of iShares Japan with Momentum plotted in the lower window. Arrow points to upside breakout from triangle pattern and corresponding increase in momentum.

Looking at the daily chart (Figure 3), EWJ drifted sideways for about a year before activity increased in August 2005. In the months preceding August, there was a classic contraction in volatility, demonstrated by the converging trendlines. Every good breakaway from a low volatility point will have either a gap or a large range increase with increasing volume. With EWJ, there was a large gap on August 10 with heavy volume. If you don't see the start of the uptrend on the chart, you certainly will on the momentum indicator (point 1), where the oscillator far exceeded its previous high points. Daily chart traders can begin to trade the pullbacks after this new momentum high.

It is important to choose ahead of time what side of the market, long or short, you will play. That's how you work most efficiently. In the case of the Japan Fund, you look to short the reactions until mid-2003, and then you look to buy the pullbacks once the trend has changed. You don't want to work both sides. Instead, work the side with the most potential gain.

Vomund: Taking advantage of pullbacks against the overall trend is an important part of your strategy. Is there a certain moving average that you like to see the security pull back to?

Raschke: Moving averages can be tools for your eye to spot pullbacks, but there isn't an optimal moving average that works best. I use a twenty-period exponential moving average as a default, though.

Vomund: At what point during a reaction against the overall trend should you enter a trade?

Raschke: That depends on how aggressive or conservative a trader you are. An aggressive trader might initiate a small-scale entry if he perceives a slowing of the reaction, whereas a conservative trader should wait until the market starts to turn back toward its trend. It also depends on the liquidity of the security. In a less liquid market, a trader will get a more advantageous price entering a long position when there are lots of sellers and vice versa. In other words, you should try to enter before the security turns, as long as you are still confident that you are trading in the direction of the higher time frame trend.

Vomund: Do you limit yourself to trading just the first two or three pullbacks, figuring that at that point a true trend reversal is due?

Raschke: You never want to limit yourself in a strongly trending market. Look at Crude Oil or Gold—there have been lots of pullbacks, but the trend is still higher. You should be careful late in the game because the security might be ripe for a bigger shakeout, but you try to differentiate whether it is a normal trading environment or if a really powerful force is at work.

It takes a lot of time to reverse a strong trend. There is usually an extended period of accumulation or distribution, so it would be extremely rare that a trend reverses on a dime without plenty of advance warning.

Trend reversals are a process that often shows up in classic chart formations like head and shoulders or broadening formations.

Vomund: Let me give you another example to look at, the iShares Russell 2000 (IWM).

Raschke: This has actually become a better trading vehicle than the Nasdaq 100 (QQQQ). Let's start with the weekly chart for IWM. Remember, weekly charts offer cleaner, prettier, and more symmetrical swings than charts with shorter time frames. Using the longer time frame, you get smoother data, less noise, and a clearer picture of the trend.

The weekly chart is in a solid uptrend where all of the upswings are greater than the downswings (Figure 4). There have been strong corrections, but the ETF remained in an uptrend. That's because for an uptrend to reverse, the security must have a lower high, a lower low, and then turn down. Because there are swings in a long-term uptrending pattern, weekly chart traders should trade the periods when the momentum indicator is increasing.

You also have to be aware of what time frame you are trading on—someone using a weekly chart will just trade long while someone using a fifteen-minute chart, although the security is in a long-term uptrend, may go short. And IWM is one of the few ETFs that can be effectively day-traded.

Looking at its fifteen-minute chart, the trend reversal that occurred in early March was a great shorting spot. In Figure 5 at point 1, the security made a lower low. The momentum oscillator at point 2 was lower than previous swings, implying the start of a bearish move. Active traders can short the pullbacks. So a day-trader can short even though longer time frames show an uptrending pattern. You have to know your time frame. You can see that fifteen-minute

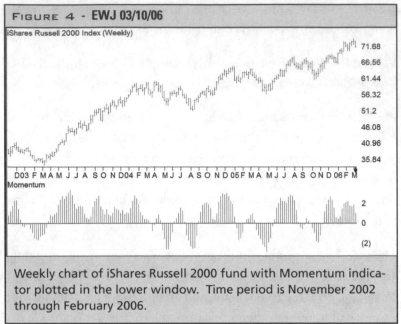

FIGURE 4 - EWJ 03/10/06

Weekly chart of iShares Russell 2000 fund with Momentum indicator plotted in the lower window. Time period is November 2002 through February 2006.

Source: AIQ Systems

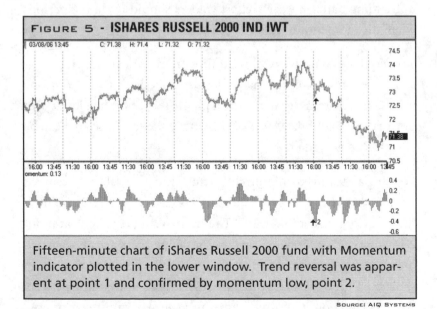

FIGURE 5 - ISHARES RUSSELL 2000 IND IWT

Fifteen-minute chart of iShares Russell 2000 fund with Momentum indicator plotted in the lower window. Trend reversal was apparent at point 1 and confirmed by momentum low, point 2.

Source: AIQ Systems

charts have a lot more noise in the data and don't have the same rhythmic swings that the weekly chart does.

Vomund: You're right when you say you are using simple classic technical analysis tools.

Raschke: I have to be honest with you; the stuff I do is so basic. However, this is what works for me. There will always be books covering new forms of technical analysis but that doesn't mean the simple classical technical analysis techniques don't work. They worked in the past, they work now, and they will work in the future.

It doesn't matter if you are a short-term aggressive professional or a longer-term investor, success depends on simply understanding the basic swings. You've noticed I'm not using fancy indicators. It is more important to simply understand the significance of the patterns, whether the security is in an uptrend with higher highs or in a downtrend with lower lows.

That's all I'm doing. I'm analyzing supply and demand shifts by the length of the swings, by whether momentum is increasing or decreasing, by whether there are higher highs or lower lows.

Vomund: Whether you use real-time, daily, or weekly charts, are there some common themes for managing a trade?

Raschke: Managing a trade means two things: placing an initial stop and following an exit strategy. Here are the common themes. Back testing and modeling price behavior shows that the great majority of the time maximum profitability is achieved by playing for small wins as opposed to shooting for a large gain. Few patterns test out where one can play for a larger gain by using a trailing stop type of strategy. Instead, our work shows that you should at least be pulling up your stop to a break-even once the trade begins to work, and then have a mechanism that forces you to take profits.

Our work shows that a combination of an initial fixed stop plus a time stop is ideal. I often employ an eight bar time stop in conjunction with a fixed stop (i.e., using a ten-minute chart you use an eighty-minute time stop, using a daily chart you use an eight-day time stop, etc.). If a trade is not working in eight bars, then it can be exited. This is true regardless of what time frame you are using.

Finally, it is important to minimize the risk of having a large loss. You don't ever want to take a large loss. Sometimes traders end up with a big loss because they were hoping for a big profit. The best traders first learn how to play good defense.

Vomund: What advice do you give to those who want to trade ETFs?

Raschke: Go to where the action is. Don't pick a dead market that isn't doing anything, hoping it will eventually break out. You have so many markets available to you that you should find choices with nice readable swings. Go to where the volatility is and where supply and demand imbalances exist. One last consideration with ETFs is relative strength work. The leaders continue to remain the leaders while the dogs will tend to continue to underperform.

For your average readers, I would also recommend to never get discouraged at the overwhelming amount of noise that there is in the market. Classic technical analysis eliminates this noise. Simply pull up charts and examine the trend, and within the trend the individual swings. You'll see they are pretty predictable. Of course it is always easier to see the swing patterns in hindsight, but with a little practice you'll identify them as they develop as well.

> You can visit Linda Bradford Raschke's web site at www.LBRgroup.com.

Vomund: Thank you for sharing your insights.

Chapter 3

Steve Palmquist & ETF Trading Techniques

S teve Palmquist is a full-time trader with twenty years of market experience who puts his own money to work in the market every day. Steve has shared trading techniques and systems with investors at seminars across the country as well as at presentations at the Traders Expo. He has published articles in *Stocks & Commodities*, *Traders-Journal*, the *AIQ Opening Bell*, and *Working Money*.

Steve has developed a market adaptive trading approach that focuses on analyzing the current market conditions and selecting the best tools to use in the current environment. He has developed and tested over a dozen different systems that along with market-driven exit strategies form the basis of his trading toolbox.

Steve is the founder of www.daisydogger.com, a web site that provides trading tips and techniques and publishes the Timely Trades Letter, which is derived from the process of writing down his market outlook, trading strategy, and trading setups prior to each trading day.

Whenever I meet an inexperienced trader I am usually asked, "What is the key to successful trading?" or "How do you pick good stocks?" Inexperienced traders are often in a never-ending search for a technique that always wins. When the technique they are using results in a few losing trades, they decide it doesn't work and move on to another. Eventually they give up or hire a fund manager. If they hire a manager, then they begin all over again—searching for the manager that always wins. There is no system that wins all the time, regardless of what the slick ads say.

The experienced trader knows that making money in the market involves knowing what to trade, when to trade, and how to change techniques and trading styles based on current market conditions. Using the same techniques and setups in all market conditions can churn your account and give you a lot of practice at taking drawdowns. The market will not adapt to us so the experienced trader learns how to adapt to the market. If you don't adapt to the market, it will eventually chew you up, along with your account.

The first step in improving trading results is to realize that the market has three modes, and we need to develop trading styles for each of these different modes. The market can be in an uptrend, defined as a set of higher highs and higher lows. It can be in a downtrend, defined as a series of lower highs and lower lows. Or it can be in a trading range, where the price oscillates between areas of support and resistance. After determining which of the three modes the market is currently in, I select one of my trading tools that has been designed for and tested under those market conditions. I also adjust my strategy for position sizing, profit taking, and number of positions in the account.

Traders, like carpenters, need to have a toolbox with more than one tool in order to get the job done. Just as a carpenter won't build a house using only a screwdriver, successful traders must pick the proper tools to use for the current market conditions. My trading toolbox consists of more than a dozen different trading techniques that have been carefully tested under each of the three market conditions. The actual trading process during market hours is the simple part of the job; successful traders put in a lot of work developing and testing systems before they ever place an order.

Trading Range

An example of a trading range market is shown in Figure 6. During the first three months of 2006, the NASDAQ traded in a range bounded by resistance in the 2330 area and support in the 2238 area. I use the NASDAQ for determining market conditions because it is representative of both big and small-cap stocks. The Dow Jones Industrial Average and the S&P 500 indexes are focused solely on

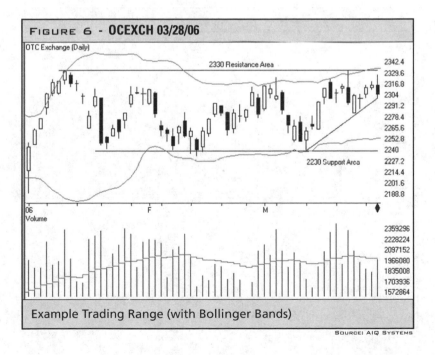

Example Trading Range (with Bollinger Bands)

SOURCE: AIQ SYSTEMS

big-cap stocks, and thus just represent a narrow slice of the overall market. The NASDAQ gives a better representation of what is going on in the overall market.

The most profitable time to trade is when the market is in a clear trend. When the market is in a trading range, it carries a little more risk. I compensate for this risk by taking smaller than normal positions. Due to the nature of a trading range, it is also important to take profits quickly. For most stocks to move a considerable distance, they need the market to be trending. In a trading range market such as Figure 6, stocks and ETFs on average tend to retrace or base sooner. This characteristic is one of the contributing factors that keep the overall market in a range.

Since ETFs tend to move shorter distances when the market is in a trading range, it makes sense to take profits quickly. An example of this is shown in Figure 7, which shows the iShares Financial

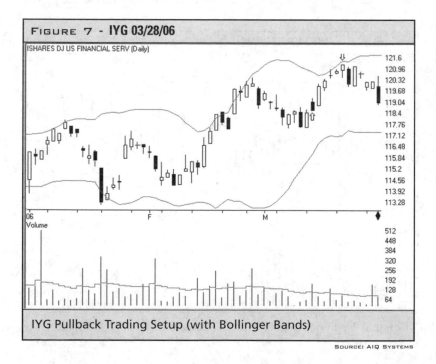

FIGURE 7 - IYG 03/28/06

IYG Pullback Trading Setup (with Bollinger Bands)

SOURCE: AIQ SYSTEMS

Services ETF (IYG) during the first three months of 2006. IYG had a nice run-up during February, reaching a peak on February 27. During the following nine sessions, it pulled back or retraced on generally below average volume. On March 13, it broke out of the pullback by forming a higher high on above average volume. The pullback pattern, consisting of a rapid price run-up followed by a low volume retracement, is one of several trading patterns that I use during trading range markets.

Note that IYG tried to break out of the pullback on March 03 and March 08 by making a higher high than the previous day, but the volume on both occasions was below average, making the pattern suspect. The breakout on March 13, noted by the up arrow in Figure 7, made a higher high than the previous day and did it on above average volume. For traders, it is very important to watch volume. Volume represents the power, or interest, behind a move.

Stocks triggering or breaking out on low volume are generally suspect. This implies that there is not much interest in the move, and if there is little interest, then the stock is less likely to keep moving. There are always counter examples, but in general I trade with the volume. I want to see stocks moving up on increasing volume and pulling back or retracing on declining volume.

I define tradable pullback patterns by a setup condition followed by a trigger condition. When the setup conditions are met, it makes the security interesting, and it goes on my watch list. When the trigger conditions are met, I enter the trade. Some setups never trigger, which is not a problem since the market always provides more interesting setups. Trading is about patterns, not particular stocks or ETFs.

The setup conditions for this type of pullback trade are a rapid price rise of at least two weeks with several above average, volume up days, followed by a pullback or retracement on generally below average volume. Stocks and ETFs that show strong gap downs or pullbacks on large volume are ignored; there are more fish in the sea.

IYG, shown in Figure 7, met these setup conditions by running up from the $114 area to the $120 area between February 08 and February 27, and after the run-up pulling back or retracing on below average volume—so it made my watch list.

Once an ETF is on my watch list, I set an alert to let me know when it has made a higher high than the previous day. The higher high is the first part of the trigger. The second part of the trigger is that the higher high occurs on increasing volume. If both these conditions are met, then I take the trade.

IYG made higher highs than the previous day on March 03 and March 08, but the volume was below average, so both trigger conditions were not met. On March 13, it made a higher high and the volume was above average, indicating that it was time to enter a position (see up arrow in Figure 7).

To use this technique one needs a way to estimate the volume on the day of the trigger. The way I do this is to recognize that there are thirteen half-hour trading periods in the trading day, and also that the volume is generally larger in the first half hour than in subsequent periods. Based on this information, I have a series of multipliers for volume based on the time of day. At the end of the first half hour of trading, I multiply the volume at that point in time by ten to estimate the volume at the end of the day. At the end of the first hour of trading, I estimate the day's volume by multiplying the current volume by 6.5. After ninety minutes of trading, I multiply the volume by 4.3, and after two hours use a multiplier of 3.2, and so on. This approach allows me to estimate a stock's or ETFs total daily volume at any interim point during the trading day.

It is not necessary to sit in front of the trading screen all day. I use an alerts screen to notify me when a setup on my watch list has made a higher high than the previous day, and then to estimate the volume using the technique outlined above. If the volume is estimated to be above average, then I have a valid trigger and can consider taking a position. Note that many brokers will email price alerts to cell phones, allowing you to trade from almost anywhere.

I do not enter a position unless I know exactly where I will exit. Immediately after entering a position, I set a stop loss order to take me out and limit my losses if the pattern fails. I also set a limit order to take me out when the stock hits a profit target. The stop loss order is always entered just under the lowest low of the setup pattern. The profit target is set at different places depending on the current market conditions.

In trading range market environments, stocks tend to make a quick move after the trigger, then pullback again or base. Because of this behavior, I typically set my limit order just under the recent high, just under the upper Bollinger Band, or under a key trendline or resistance level. I do not enter orders for even numbers or numbers ending in five, since that is where most people enter and I want my order to be just under where the crowd has theirs.

In the case of IYG (Figure 7), the low of the setup pattern was $117.50 on March 07, so the stop should be set just under this level at $117.39. If the setup fails and price reaches a lower low, then the pattern will be invalidated, and I no longer want to be in the position. My risk on the trade is the difference between the trigger price and the stop loss. Remember, the trigger occurred on March 13 when IYG moved above the previous day's high on above average volume. Since the previous day's high was $118.60, my risk on the trade is $118.60 minus $117.39, or $1.21.

I use the amount at risk, $1.21, to help determine how many shares to buy. If I am willing to risk $500 on each trade, then I can buy 500 divided by 1.21, or 413 shares. Each trader has different account sizes and financial situations and thus is willing to risk different amounts on each trade. Determining the maximum amount you are willing to risk on each trade is an important part of trading.

Trading is a statistical business, where it is important to have a system that wins more often than it loses, and the average winning trade gains more than the average losing trade loses. If these conditions are met, then averaged over the long term, the system is likely to be profitable. Any single trade may or may not be profitable, but after a number of trades, the statistics should prove out and the system should show a profit. Recognizing the statistical nature of trading is one of the keys to success.

Traders who risk half their account size on each trade may see some spectacular returns in the short run, but are highly likely to go broke in the long run. There are old traders and bold traders, but few old bold traders.

> The market does not care about random numbers or percentages, but it does care about patterns.

Let's assume that with a large number of trades, a system can show eight losing trades in a row. If that is the case, I want to be able to take this hit without risking my account or becoming emotional. I use this information to determine the maximum amount I am willing to risk on any single trade. If a $12,000 drawdown would not risk a trader's account or cause him to lose sleep, then the most he should be willing to risk on any single trade would be $12,000 divided by eight, or $1,500.

In the case of the IYG trade, the spread between the trigger and the stop loss was $1.21, so the number of shares to trade would be 1,500 divided by 1.21, or 1,239 shares. In practice, I round these share numbers to the nearest hundred.

Remember, the stop loss is placed under the low of the setup pattern, not some random number or percentage. The market does not care about random numbers or percentages, but it does care about patterns. Let the pattern determine the stop loss, and let the maximum amount you are willing to risk on any single trade determine the number of shares to buy.

After placing the stop order under the low of the setup pattern, I enter a sell limit order at a profit target. In trading range markets, I am looking to take profits quickly, so the limit order is usually placed just under the high of the setup pattern, or just under the upper Bollinger Band. In the case of the IYG trade shown in Figure 7, I placed the limit order under the Bollinger Band at $120.74.

The limit order was hit on the fourth day of the trade resulting in a profit of $120.74 minus $118.60, or $2.14. IYG moved to a new high of $121.20 two days later (see down arrow on Figure 7), then started another pullback to a low of $118.65 on March 29. Forget about getting out at the exact high; it can't be done consistently. However, this technique captured most of the move and resulted in a much better profit than if we had held for another two weeks.

When the market is oscillating between support and resistance, traders should focus on taking quick profits and moving on to the next trade. Making a number of small profits during a trading range market can be much more profitable than blindly buying and holding, hoping for the best. Hope is not a trading technique, taking profits is. Letting positions run and longer-term holding are for trending market environments, not trading range markets.

With stocks and ETFs that trade on low volume (less than 100,000 shares a day), I will consider using a mental stop rather than entering the stop order. Very low volume securities can sometimes be manipulated, so caution is warranted. With higher volume securities, I usually enter on a market order. With low volume securities, I always use a limit order to enter a new position.

The OCO, or "order cancels order," entry is ideal for traders. After taking a trade I enter both the stop and the limit orders using this order type. If either one is executed, then the other order is cancelled. This allows me to take a trade, enter the exit parameters, and let the broker's computer keep an eye on things for me while I do something else. Most brokers offer the OCO trade entry. If yours doesn't, consider changing brokers.

Figure 8 shows another example of trading pullback setups during a trading range market environment. In Figure 8, iShares Healthcare (IYH) showed a nice run-up between February 07, 2006 and February 27, 2006, then pulled back or retraced for six sessions. As IYH started pulling back after the run-up, it made my watch list as an interesting setup. On March 08, it moved above the previous day's high of $64.15 on above average volume, which constituted a trigger condition (see arrows).

When IYH triggered on good volume, the trade could be entered at $64.20, slightly above the previous day's high. After entering the

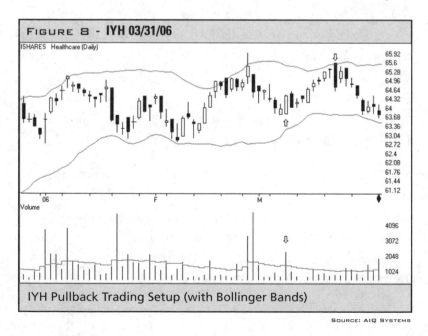

IYH Pullback Trading Setup (with Bollinger Bands)

trade, a stop should be placed under the low of the setup pattern. The low of the pattern was $63.75 on March 07, so a stop order was entered for $63.64 to protect against pattern failure.

The difference between the entry at $64.20 and the stop at $63.64 was $0.56. If the maximum amount a trader is willing to risk on any single trade is $500, then the amount purchased should be 500 divided by 0.56, or 892 shares. Along with the stop order entry, a limit order should be set at a profit target, which in this case would be just under the upper Bollinger Band—$65.49 on the day of the trigger. I would use a limit order of $65.39.

After the trigger, IYH continued to move up and hit the $65.39 level on the eighth day of the trade, causing the limit order to be executed. It reached a high for this run the following day and then started an eight-day pullback that took it back under the trigger price. Holding this stock for sixteen days would have resulted in no gain. Using the techniques outlined above resulted in a profit of $1.19 in eight days. A 2 % profit in eight days keeps food on the table; repeating this a number of times during a trading range market puts money in the bank.

Trending Markets

Trading range markets do not last forever. Eventually the market will break above resistance or below support. When this happens, I start looking for signs that the market is establishing a trend, defined as a series of higher highs and higher lows (uptrend) or a series of lower lows and lower highs (downtrend). Trending markets can be quite profitable for traders because they represent less risk than trading range markets and positions may be held longer.

One of the keys to trading is to adjust the position sizing and holding times for trades depending on the market conditions. In trading range markets, I often use half-size positions and holding times may be measured in days. In trending markets, I use full-size positions and holding times may be measured in weeks. This is part of adapting to the market. Trading the same way in all market conditions is likely to just churn your account.

It is amazing how many people tell me they are short-term traders, or swing traders, or long-term traders. You can't decide what you're going to be, then force your ideas on the market. You must look at what the market is doing, and then pick a style that is profitable for the current conditions. If the market is range bound, I will be a short-term or a swing trader. If the market is strongly trending, I will hold longer and take larger positions. My style of trading is determined by the market. If you use the same style all the time, you are likely to eventually take a hit. Adapt to the market—it will not adapt to you.

Figure 9 shows a period between October 15, 2004 and January 04, 2005 when the market was in an up trend. The market was in a

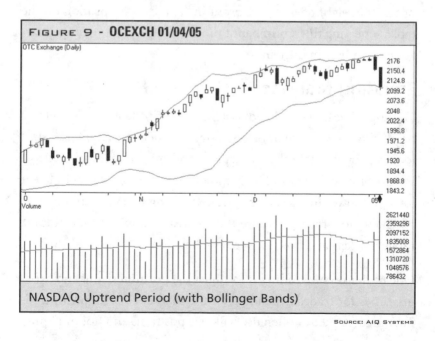

FIGURE 9 - OCEXCH 01/04/05

OTC Exchange (Daily)

NASDAQ Uptrend Period (with Bollinger Bands)

small basing area during the middle of October. It broke above this basing area on October 27, 2004 and continued to make a series of higher highs and higher lows for the remainder of the year. When the market is trending, I give my trades more room to run and take larger positions than I do in a trading range market.

When the market is trending, I also trade more types of patterns. For example, base breakouts are usually not interesting in a trading range market, but are one of the patterns I look for when the market is trending. As shown in Figure 10, iShares Technology (IYW) had formed a narrow base during October. On October 28, 2004, IYW moved above the top of the recent range on twice-average volume (see arrow). Since volume measures the pressure behind or interest in a move, the break from a trading range on twice-average volume is a significant event.

Imagine you are running a clothing store, and you have a rack of red shirts and another rack of green shirts. During the last month, you have been selling a few of each kind at the same price. One day there is a run on red shirts, and you sell out. Which do you order more of? Obviously, there is a strong and sudden demand for red shirts, so you want to have more of them around to meet the new demand.

Does it matter to you why red shirts are suddenly selling? No, you are just in a hurry to get more. You are also likely to realize that if red shirts are suddenly in demand, you can likely charge more for them, so you raise the price. High demand leads to higher prices. When there isn't demand for something, the price drops. The slow moving shirts are put on sale to clear the inventory.

The same supply and demand issues drive the stock market. During the month of October, there was light demand for IYW. On October 28, suddenly twice as many people wanted it. It doesn't matter why. The point is; it's selling fast just like the red shirts. The demand has increased, and so the price is likely to increase also.

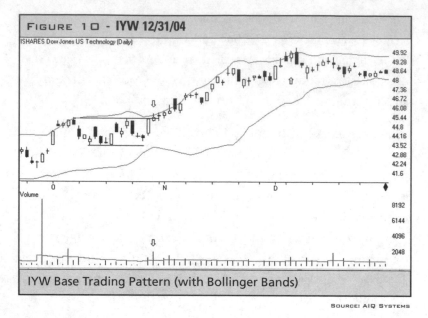

FIGURE 1 0 - **IYW 12/31/04**

ISHARES Dow Jones US Technology (Daily)

IYW Base Trading Pattern (with Bollinger Bands)

When a security is in a trading range, it indicates that most people believe it is fairly priced. Supply and demand are roughly equal. When it breaks above the trading range on strong volume, it indicates that a lot more buyers have come in and are willing to pay more for the security. They believe it is undervalued and are picking it up. Dollars are votes—they are voting to raise the price of the security. When the market is in an uptrend, I may enter ETFs and stocks that are breaking out of basing areas.

After breaking out of a basing area on October 28, IYW ran up for another month. During favorable market conditions, ETFs tend to run longer, so I increase my holding time and also my position sizes for each trade. During trending markets, I do not take profits as positions hit the upper Bollinger Band because, instead of dropping back, they tend to "ride" the bands.

In trending markets, I use topping patterns and trendlines to determine when to exit positions. Double tops, head and shoulders, rat tails, and volume distribution patterns offer good clues that it is time to exit a position. A distribution day occurs when the stock is down on volume larger than the pervious day. I have found that an occasional distribution day is not necessarily significant, but my research indicates that three distribution days in the past ten sessions is a good indicator that the current run may be ending. If I see three distribution days in the past ten sessions, then I need a very good reason to continue holding the position.

"Rat tails" occur when the stock runs up well past the open then pulls back to close near, or even below, the opening price. On a candlestick chart, these are shown as long upper shadows. They happen because the stock was bid up significantly during the day but then ran into selling pressure and pulled back. When this happens repeatedly, it shows a lack of strength. When a stock shows a lack of strength, I exit the position and move on to another. I want to take profits as a stock's run weakens and move my money into something that is stronger or just starting its run. Remember the red shirts.

On the IYW chart (Figure 10), "rat tails" appear three days in a row in early December, as marked by the up arrow. When I see this kind of pattern after a nice run, I exit the position. IYW had run up for about a month before showing the "rat tails," so when I saw them, it was clear that something was changing, and it was time to exit the position and move on. The "rat tail" pattern was in fact the peak for IYW, and it began a slow decline that took it back below the initial base breakout in late January.

A "buy and holder" who took a position during the breakout in late October would have seen a nice profit by early December, then would have watched it turn into a loss by late January. In fact, it would take another year for the price to return to the highs reached in early December. The market generally gives good clues on when to get in and when to get out. Buy and hold equals buy and hope,

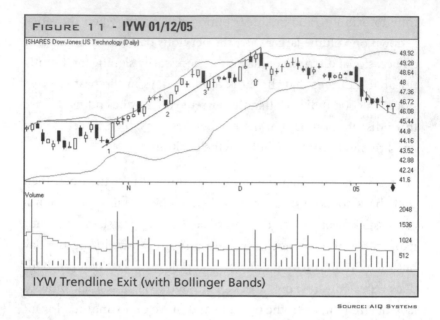

FIGURE 11 - IYW 01/12/05

ISHARES Dow Jones US Technology (Daily)

IYW Trendline Exit (with Bollinger Bands)

SOURCE: AIQ SYSTEMS

and hope is not a trading strategy. Rather than buy and hope, I enter when the security shows increased interest in bidding up the price and exit when topping patterns indicate the process may reverse. Rather than tying up my money for long periods, I enter and exit based on trading patterns. When one pattern is complete, I move on to the next one.

I also closely monitor trendlines as one of my exit strategies during trending markets. Trendlines are simple, basic, and functional. If you don't have a couple on your chart, then you may be making a mistake.

Figure 11 shows how I would use a trendline to exit the IYW trade. After entering the IYW trade on the high volume base breakout of October 28, I was looking for a light volume pullback at some point to establish a higher low. IYW continued to run through early November on good volume after the base. During the second week of November, it dropped slightly on below average volume and then quickly moved back up to form new highs. This low volume pullback resulted in a higher high after the pullback, and a higher low formed during the pullback process.

The pattern of higher highs and higher lows is by definition an uptrend. During uptrends I draw an ascending trendline under the higher lows and use breaks of this trendline as possible exit points. In the case of IYW, I drew an ascending trendline between the low of the setup pattern, shown as point 1 in Figure 11, and the first higher low, shown as point 2. As long as the ETF is above this trendline, I am happy to let my profits run. A break below this trendline would be a warning that something is changing, and I would consider taking profits.

IYW broke the ascending trendline at point 3 on Figure 11. If I took profits at point 3, I would have captured much of the move. The trendline break exit approach does not capture as much of the run as the "rat tail" approach outlined above does, but it results in a nice profit and allows the money to work elsewhere two weeks earlier. There is nothing wrong with taking some profits early, but there is a problem with holding on too long and letting a winning position turn into a loser.

Some traders combine the approaches: taking profits on half the position on the trendline break, moving the stop on the remaining shares up to at least break even, and letting them run while monitoring the stock for a topping pattern. Any one of these three approaches can work. The key is to have a clearly defined approach and not just hold on hoping for more.

Volume patterns are something I am always keenly aware of when trading. The ideal ETF runs up on high volume and pulls back or declines on low volume. When I see a security dropping on large volume, it flashes a caution sign. When this happens several times in a few days, then I am interested in exiting the position and looking for another. If the security is dropping on large volume, then there are a lot of people who are willing to sell their holdings for less than they were worth the day before. If a lot of people are suddenly willing to take less for the security, then I want to dump it and find something for which a lot of people are willing to pay more.

Figure 12 illustrates how volume patterns may be used for exiting positions. PowerShares Dynamic Market Portfolio (PWC) pulled back during the first three weeks of October 2005. It broke out of the pullback pattern on October 26 on well above average volume (see arrow). The pullback setup would trigger on the move above $35.35, on October 26. After entering a position, the protective stop for pattern failure would be under the low of the pattern that was $34.87 on October 20, just four days before the trigger.

Since the market was in an uptrend during this period, I would not exit at the upper Bollinger Band. Instead, I watch for signs of a topping pattern. PWC continued to move up through the first half of November. In mid-November, PWC showed two distribution days

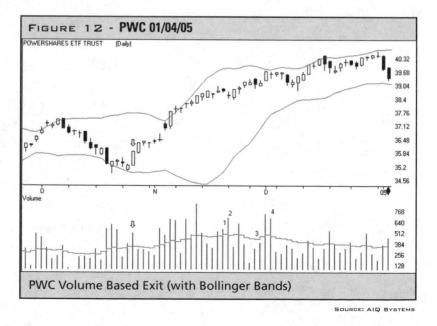

FIGURE 12 - PWC 01/04/05

PWC Volume Based Exit (with Bollinger Bands)

marked as points 1 and 2 on Figure 12. Two distribution days are the market's way of getting your attention and signaling that caution is appropriate.

Five days after the first distribution, PWC showed another distribution day (point 3 in Figure 12) and three days after that PWC showed another high volume down day (point 4). At that point, it's time to exit the stock and put the money to work in something that is showing signs of strength, not weakness. This exit was triggered around $39.60. Three weeks later the stock hit its high for the run at $40.48. Rather than waiting around another three weeks for the last few cents in the run, the volume pattern got traders out near the top and let them put their money to work in a stronger setup.

> Distribution day is when the security closes down with volume heavier than the previous day's volume

Finally, in trending markets I will buy flag patterns without waiting for a trigger above the top of the flag. This is because in a trending market, flags are usually continuation patterns, and when they move, they move quickly.

Summary

I can't control what the market does, so I have a plan for whichever path it takes—and then trade the plan. As a trader, I do not care which way the market moves; I can make money either way. The only disappointing periods are the occasional times when the market trades in a very narrow trading range. It is important to be able to quickly react to what the market does and not be emotionally attached to any particular choice.

Narrow trading ranges are best avoided because there isn't enough time for swing trades to work. Fortunately, narrow ranges do not happen often. The best time for trading is when the market is in a clear trend, or a wide trading range that takes at least a week to move from one end to the other. In a trending market, I will lengthen holding times and give my holdings more room to run. In a wide trading range or an uncertain market, I use short holding times and grab profits quickly.

It is important to wait for the triggers for most patterns and not jump the gun and get in too early. Pullbacks in trending stocks may be a normal pause, or the end of the trend. When the stock pulls back for a few days and either moves above the previous day's high or breaks above the trendline drawn across the tops of the highs of the pullback, it is not likely to be the end of the trend. It is more likely that the trend has resumed.

Stops are important and should be set based on the chart pattern, not some random point or dollar figure. I generally set them just under the lowest low of the setup. If the spread between the stop point and the entry point is more risk than I am willing to take for a given number of shares, I pass on the trade.

Yes, I occasionally watch CNBC, usually when there is a major news event that interests me. Watching CNBC is more likely to cost me money rather than make me money because the network's job is to sell commercials, not provide actionable data. Stocks trade based on supply and demand, which is shown in the charts, not some analyst's opinion. The analysts rarely agree with each other, leading to confusion. The charts show how people are voting with real dollars and provide actionable information.

If you would like to see a sample of Steve Palmquist's current market outlook and the trading setups he is currently watching, send a request to ETF@daisydogger.com.

Be guided by the market not the opinions or hopes of others. Learn to read the NASDAQ and focus most of your trading on the times when it is bouncing off support or resistance. If you don't have a reasonable idea of where the market is headed, don't trade until it becomes clearer. Always be thinking about taking and protecting profits.

Part III

MECHANICAL ROTATION STRATEGIES

Part III presents several fully mechanical ETF rotation models. While one model requires a custom formula to determine rotation timing, other models use simple price rate of change calculations that can be applied by anyone.

The models are simple, easy to follow, and effective. They are based on the assumption that in most market environments, there is an area of leadership. Our models rotate to the leadership segments. The models are designed for different ETF categories that include style, sector, and international ETFs.

Many of our reader's portfolios will have a trading component and a long-term growth component. This section's mechanical rotation strategies are designed for long-term growth. They are based on the simple assumption that over the long run, stocks go up. History bears this out.

From 1928 through 2005, stocks gained an average of 11.7% per year. That's well ahead of the 3.9% gain in T-Bills and 5.2% gain in T-Bonds. Stocks don't increase in a straight line, however. Over those seventy-eight years, there were only six years when the market's gain came within 3% of its historical average!

While stock returns vary greatly over short time periods, their return becomes very predictable over longer periods. In his book, *The Future For Investors*, Jeremy Siegel found that the historical after-inflation return on stocks is 6.5% to 7%. That is true for the early U.S. economic development from 1802 to 1870, for the middle period of 1871 to 1926, and from 1926 through 2003, which includes the great depression, wars, and terrorism. A 6.5 to 7% after-inflation return means an investor's wealth doubles on average every decade.

Institutional investors know the market increases over the long run. That's why the Vanguard Index 500, which tracks the S&P 500 index, is the largest mutual fund. Still, returns can be greatly increased by not limiting yourself to one market index. The Style Index strategy that we will outline is an active indexing strategy, which involves buying the best performing U.S. market indexes. It is also a groundbreaking strategy, since trading vehicles that track the style indexes weren't available until 2001.

We'll also apply the market rotation techniques to the more aggressive sector and international ETFs.

Presented in Part III are back tests of mechanical strategies, representing paper portfolio returns. It should be noted, however, that my managed account company (www.ETFportfolios.net) has traded the style index choices for over three years and the returns are very similar to the back tested returns.

Chapter 4

Market Rotation Strategy

Most investors are comfortable with their approaches; ones they insist work best over the long term. Value investors stay the course even when a growth approach outperforms for several years, and growth managers do the same when the opposite is true. Small-cap investors keep their focus even when large-cap stocks are leading the way. Large-cap investors do the same when small caps do well. Unfortunately, market environments change and few investors adjust to the rotation.

Market Rotation

Let's look more closely at market rotation. In 1994 through 1999, the Nasdaq Composite, a good measure of growth stocks, had an average gain of 32% per year. The S&P 500 Value Index lagged with its 16% annual rate of return. This was a great time for growth investors.

Just when most people employed growth strategies, the market environment dramatically changed. From 2000 through 2004 the Nasdaq Composite lost 12% annually. Investors who stuck with their growth-based strategies were crushed. Value investors, however, didn't feel the sting of the bear market. The S&P 500 Value Index gained 0.5% annually.

The same type of rotation also occurs with large-cap and small-cap stocks. From 1998 through 1999, the S&P 500, a measure of large-company stocks, gained 23% annually. The Russell 2000, a measure of small-company stocks, lagged with a 7.5% annual return. Large-cap fund managers did very well during this period while small-cap managers underperformed.

The opposite was true in 2000 through 2005. Small-cap stocks as measured by the Russell 2000 gained 4.9% annually while the S&P 500 lost 2.7% annually. Investors who concentrated on small-cap stocks saw their portfolios hitting new all-time highs in 2005 while large-cap investors were still 20% below the March 2000 high.

Instead of locking into one trading style, it is best to employ a strategy that rotates to the best performing segment. That's what our market rotation strategies are all about.

The rotation strategies trade ETFs that track various market indexes. We'll begin with "style" indexes. Style indexes include large-cap growth, large-cap value, small-cap growth, small-cap value, and so forth. When large-cap stocks outperform, the systems are designed to rotate to ETFs that track a large-cap index. Similarly, when growth stocks outperform, the systems are designed to rotate to growth-oriented ETFs.

Rather than guessing what market segment will outperform, we let the market tell us when to rotate.

Strategy Back Test

In order to develop systematic trading models, we need to be able to run back tests that cover several market cycles. That's hard to do with ETFs because their price history is so limited. Most ETFs were introduced in 2000 or later so running a back test that includes the bull market of the 1990s is impossible.

To get around this, we ran models on the benchmark indexes that the ETFs track during time periods when the ETFs didn't exist.

Here's an example. Before the Nasdaq 100 ETF (QQQQ) was introduced for trading, our back test purchased the Nasdaq 100 index. Before the Dow Diamond (DIA) was introduced, the back test bought the Dow Jones Industrial Average. Before the iShares Small-Cap Russell 2000 was introduced, the back test bought the Russell 2000 index. A list of the ETFs used in the initial back tests along with their benchmark indexes is found in Table 1.

Ticker	ETF	Benchmark Index
DIA	Diamond	Dow Jones Industrial Avg.
QQQQ	Nasdaq 100 Tracking Stock	Nasdaq 100
SPY	S&P 500 SPDR	S&P 500
MDY	MidCap SPDR	S&P MidCap
IJS	iShares Small-Cap Value	S&P 600 SmallCap/ BARRA Value
IJT	iShares Small-Cap Growth	S&P 600 SmallCap/ BARRA Growth
IWM	iShares Small-Cap Index	Russell 2000

Table 1 - Market Segment ETF Choices
A list of ETFs along with their benchmark indexes.

Our first model, the Basic Rotation model, is a simple but highly effective rotation strategy that buys the best performing ETFs as measured over the previous six-month period. The ETFs included in this model are the same as those listed in Table 1.

Most every analysis software package will allow you to calculate six-month returns (approximately 120 trading days). You can also get six-month returns free at www.bigcharts.com. To see the best performers on this web site, chart all the ETFs using a six-month time period. We also post returns at www.ETFtradingstrategies.com.

In our back tests, the portfolios were always fully invested in two ETFs or equivalent indexes and rebalanced at the end of every year, giving the two securities an equal weighting. We rebalanced the account each year to better see how the strategy performed on a yearly basis, but the rebalancing lowered the overall return. Rebalancing forces you to partially sell your best holdings.

In the back tests, positions were bought and sold on the day a switch is indicated and a $17 commission was applied. Dividends were excluded from both the ETF and S&P 500's returns.

Basic Rotation Strategy

We began the test of our Basic Rotation system at the start of the first month by running a six-month price change report on the ETFs shown in Table 1. To establish a fully invested portfolio, the two best-performing ETFs were purchased with equal dollar amounts. These two ETFs were held through the remainder of the month.

At the start of the next month, the six-month price changes were computed again. As long as the current holdings were among the top three performers, then there were no changes. If a holding was not one of the three best six-month performers, then it was sold and the best performer was purchased. We never doubled into a position.

Let's clarify this with an example. Figure 13 shows the six-month price change report at the start of February. Looking at the report, which is ranked in the order of six-month performance, it is apparent that small-company stocks are leading while large-company stocks are underperforming. The portfolio begins by investing in the top two performers; iShares Russell 2000 (IWM) and S&P Mid-Cap 400 SPDR (MDY).

IWM and MDY are held throughout February and on March 1, a new six-month price change report is computed (Figure 14). Since both IWM and MDY are among the top three performers, there are no trades. This process is repeated at the start of every month.

FIGURE 13 - AIQ REPORTS

Reports   View   Generate   Help

Upside Price Change Report
02/01/06 — Daily
Short Term

Ticker	Stock	Percent	Price
IWM	iShares Russell 2000 Index	11	73.10
MDY	S & P Midcap 400	10	142.97
IJS	iShares S&P Smallcap 600 Value	10	69.94
IJT	iShares S&P Smallcap 600 Growth	9	125.13
QQQQ	Nasdaq 100 Tracking Stock	8	42.15
IVE	iShares S&P 500 Value	5	67.25
SPY	S&P 500 Spyder	4	128.39

120-day Price Change report on February 1, 2006. The report was run on list of ETFs and shows a small-cap and a mid-cap ETF, IWM and MDY, in top positions.

Source: AIQ Systems

FIGURE 14 - AIQ REPORTS

Reports   View   Generate   Help

Upside Price Change Report
03/01/06 — Daily
Short Term

Ticker	Stock	Percent	Price
IWM	iShares Russell 2000 Index	10	73.90
MDY	S & P Midcap 400	9	143.67
IJS	iShares S&P Smallcap 600 Value	9	70.58
IJT	iShares S&P Smallcap 600 Growth	8	125.11
IVE	iShares S&P 500 Value	6	68.33
QQQQ	Nasdaq 100 Tracking Stock	6	41.66
SPY	S&P 500 Spyder	4	129.37

A 120-day Price Change report on March 1, 2006. IWM and MDY remain the two best performers.

Source: AIQ Systems

Results

The strategy is designed to rotate to the segments of the market with the best performance. It works. The yearly results are shown in Table 2. The strategy outperformed the S&P 500 during the up years. With that said, one would expect the strategy to fall faster than the S&P 500 during the down years. Not so.

After the technology bubble burst in 2000, the portfolio outperformed because it exited the volatile Nasdaq 100 ETF and rotated to small and mid-cap ETFs. Small-cap stocks actually rose in value during 2001. It continued to benefit from small-cap holdings in the remaining years.

Year	Basic Rotation (%)	S&P 500 Index (%)
1998	44.25	26.67
1999	57.85	19.53
2000	5.80	-10.14
2001	-2.23	-13.04
2002	-17.85	-23.37
2003	43.29	26.38
2004	13.01	8.99
2005	3.92	3.00
2006 *	12.64	3.73
AROI	16.91	3.56

Table 2 - Basic Rotation Strategy Yearly Returns
4 1/4 round trip trades per year. Average holding period of 179 days.
Through March 31, 2006

Over this period, the Basic Rotation strategy had a 16.91% average annual rate of return (267% total gain) compared to just a 3.6% annual gain in the S&P 500 and a 4.9% annual gain in the Nasdaq Composite (Figure 15). A listing of the individual trades can be found at www.ETFtradingstrategies.com.

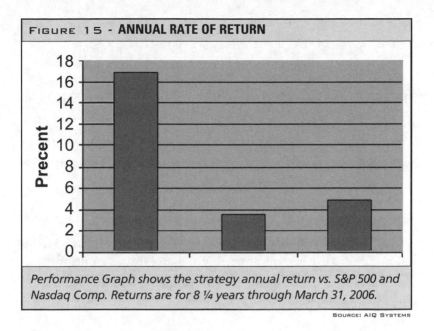

FIGURE 15 - **ANNUAL RATE OF RETURN**

Precent

18
16
14
12
10
8
6
4
2
0

Performance Graph shows the strategy annual return vs. S&P 500 and Nasdaq Comp. Returns are for 8 ¼ years through March 31, 2006.

SOURCE: AIQ SYSTEMS

These returns come with amazingly few trades. The average holding period is 179 days. This was an especially good time period for this strategy as several holdings were held for long periods (expect a little more trading as we move forward). Still, this is ideal for longer-term investors who are willing to perform a simple analysis once a month.

While this is a hypothetical back test and past performance does not guarantee future results, one can see that by making a simple evaluation once a month and then rotating to the best performing market segments, one can significantly outperform a buy-and-hold strategy. For a detailed listing of the assumptions behind the test, see Part III Conclusion.

Style Index Strategy

An effective trading strategy is only good if you can follow it. Although the Basic Rotation strategy is extremely effective and simple to apply, I would have a hard time placing client money in it.

During uncertain times (which is all the time!), it would be hard to rotate to a volatile ETF like the Nasdaq 100 ETF (QQQQ) at the start of the month knowing that I'm locked into it for the entire month.

If I'm going to second guess trades or hold off placing them, then I'm not following the strategy and in the long run, returns will be compromised. To rectify this, I've made two modifications to the Basic Rotation model to make it more comfortable to follow. The result is our Style Index strategy.

The first change is that we'll evaluate rotation every other week instead of once a month. I can buy the Nasdaq 100 ETF (QQQQ) knowing that if I bought at the high, then I'll rotate out of it just two weeks later. That's easier to swallow than holding a losing security for an entire month.

The second change is that when we evaluate its six-month performance, we'll place more emphasis on recent performance compared to what happened six months ago. To do this, break the six-month time period into four equal parts (i.e., about thirty trading days). Calculate a percentage change for each period and then average them, placing twice the weight on the most recent period.

Calculating relative strength in this manner can be done in most analysis software packages. We used a pre-built report in AIQ's TradingExpert Pro software package (www.aiqsystems.com). We also post similar calculations at www.ETFtradingstrategies.com.

Applying these two changes doesn't increase the overall return from the system, but it makes the system more comfortable to apply and, therefore, more likely that you will follow the system's signals.

The trading approach is similar to that shown in the Basic Rotation model, but we'll apply our two modifications. To begin our Style Index rotation system, a six-month relative strength report that places the most emphasis on what has happened recently was run on the ETFs in Table 1. At the start of the test, the two best-performing ETFs were purchased with equal dollar amounts to establish a fully invested portfolio. Two weeks later, a six-month relative strength report was run again. If the current holdings were in the top half of the report (i.e., one of the three best performers), then there were no trades. If a holding fell in the relative strength report ranking and was no longer in the top three, then it was sold and the highest-rated ETF was purchased. We never doubled into a current holding.

Figure 16 shows the relative strength report on January 06. Looking at the report, The Nasdaq 100 Tracking Stock (QQQQ) and the S&P Mid-Cap SPDR (MDY) are the two best performers, so they are purchased to create a fully invested portfolio.

Two weeks later, the relative strength report is calculated again (Figure 17). Notice the Nasdaq 100 ETF fell to the bottom half of the report. It is sold and the proceeds enter the iShares Russell 2000 (IWM). This process is repeated every other week.

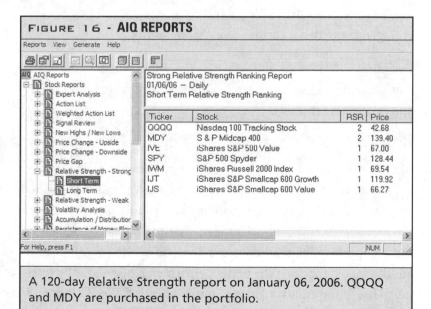

FIGURE 16 - AIQ REPORTS

Strong Relative Strength Ranking Report
01/06/06 — Daily
Short Term Relative Strength Ranking

Ticker	Stock	RSR	Price
QQQQ	Nasdaq 100 Tracking Stock	2	42.68
MDY	S & P Midcap 400	2	139.40
IVE	iShares S&P 500 Value	1	67.00
SPY	S&P 500 Spyder	1	128.44
IWM	iShares Russell 2000 Index	1	69.54
IJT	iShares S&P Smallcap 600 Growth	1	119.92
IJS	iShares S&P Smallcap 600 Value	1	66.27

A 120-day Relative Strength report on January 06, 2006. QQQQ and MDY are purchased in the portfolio.

SOURCE: AIQ SYSTEMS

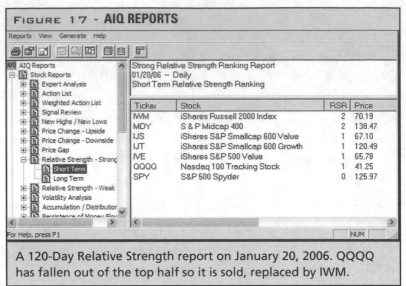

FIGURE 17 - AIQ REPORTS

Reports View Generate Help

AIQ Reports
- Stock Reports
  - Expert Analysis
  - Action List
  - Weighted Action List
  - Signal Review
  - New Highs / New Lows
  - Price Change - Upside
  - Price Change - Downside
  - Price Gap
  - Relative Strength - Strong
    - Short Term
    - Long Term
  - Relative Strength - Weak
  - Volatility Analysis
  - Accumulation / Distribution
  - Persistence of Money Flow

Strong Relative Strength Ranking Report
01/20/06 — Daily
Short Term Relative Strength Ranking

Ticker	Stock	RSR	Price
IWM	iShares Russell 2000 Index	2	70.19
MDY	S & P Midcap 400	2	138.47
IJS	iShares S&P Smallcap 600 Value	1	67.10
IJT	iShares S&P Smallcap 600 Growth	1	120.49
IVE	iShares S&P 500 Value	1	65.78
QQQQ	Nasdaq 100 Tracking Stock	1	41.25
SPY	S&P 500 Spyder	0	125.97

For Help, press F1 — NUM

A 120-Day Relative Strength report on January 20, 2006. QQQQ has fallen out of the top half so it is sold, replaced by IWM.

SOURCE: AIQ SYSTEMS

As in the back test, ETFs were purchased when they were available. Before the ETF was introduced, however, their benchmark indexes were bought and sold. The portfolio was always fully invested in two ETFs or equivalent indexes and rebalanced at the end of every year, giving the two securities an equal weighting.

Positions were bought and sold the day of the signal, and a $17 commission was used. Dividends were excluded from both the ETF and S&P 500's returns.

Results

Many people follow an indexing strategy, knowing that the market increases in the long run. That's why the Vanguard Index 500 mutual fund has more assets than any other fund. Our Style Index strategy applies this concept but says that the S&P 500 isn't always the best performing market index. Sometimes the Russell 2000 or another market index is the better performer. By periodically rotating to the leading market indexes, returns are well above a buy-and-hold strategy (Table 3).

Year	Basic Rotation (%)	S&P 500 Index (%)
1998	41.80	26.67
1999	61.73	19.53
2000	-2.25	-10.14
2001	-3.09	-13.04
2002	-14.90	-23.37
2003	43.43	26.38
2004	12.08	8.99
2005	-1.89	3.00
2006 *	10.46	3.73
AROI	15.20	3.56

Table 3 - Style Index Strategy Yearly Returns
10 round trip trades per year. Average holding period of 74 days.
Through May 31, 2006

This is an easy strategy to apply. Rotation is evaluated every other week and more oftentimes trades are not needed. During this 8 ¼-year test, there was an average of ten round-trip trades per year, or an average holding period of seventy-four days.

Some people discount this approach because of its simplicity. This simplicity, however, is what makes it attractive. Complex systems work for a year or two and then begin to fail. With the Style Index strategy, when an area of the market assumes market leadership and outperforms, then the strategy benefits by rotating to that area.

For details on every transaction and updated performance statistics, visit www.ETFtradingstrategies.com. Past performance does not guarantee future results. For other important assumptions, see Part III Conclusion.

Summary

Both the Basic Rotation and Style Index Rotation models effectively take advantage of the normal rotation within the market. You can employ either strategy and expect to outperform the market, or you can run a portfolio that utilizes both methods.

Please place a bookmark on these Style Index results as the next few chapters will show variations to this model and returns will be compared.

Chapter 5

Types of Variations

Variation #1 – Rotate Every Week

When we present the Style Index portfolio method to investment groups, they inevitability ask what happens when you make variations to the trading model. In our first variation, we'll run the Style Index relative strength report every week (as opposed to every other week) looking for possible rotation. Except for this variation, the methodology outlined in the Style Index section of Chapter 4 applies.

The yearly back test results are found in Table 4. The yearly returns are very similar to the original Style Index returns in Chapter 4, but the overall return is slightly higher. This is a bit overstated as the number of trades has increased. If slippage were factored in, the overall return would likely be closer to the return in the original Style Index strategy.

Year	Basic Rotation (%)	S&P 500 Index (%)
1998	40.06	26.67
1999	57.74	19.53
2000	2.19	-10.14
2001	0.36	-13.04

2002	-16.69	-23.37
2003	41.84	26.38
2004	15.04	8.99
2005	2.60	3.00
2006 *	10.65	3.73
AROI	16.35	3.56

Table 4 - Style Index Variation #1 – Weekly Rotation
12 round trip trades per year. Average holding period of 61 days.
Through March 31, 2006

For details on every transaction and updated performance statistics, visit www.ETFtradingstrategies.com. Past performance does not guarantee future results. For other important assumptions, see Part III Conclusion.

Summary

I'm not willing to trade more if the system doesn't get you in earlier in an uptrend and out earlier in a downtrend. While this variation may be a better fit for some of our readers, I'm not willing to increase the trading for about the same overall return.

Variation #2 – Adding a Bond Fund

The next variation to the original Style Index strategy is to add a bond fund to the ETF choices found in Table 1(page 47). Since no ETF bond fund dates back to 1997, as a proxy, we used the Vanguard Long Term U.S. Bond Fund (VUSTX). It is reasonable to assume that an ETF bond fund would have similar movement.

We used the same trading methodology as the Style Index strategy with one exception; by adding a bond fund, there were eight ETF choices. Our goal is to own ETFs in the top half of the report; so as long as current holdings are in the top four positions of the relative strength report, then there are no trades (as opposed to the top three positions in the original Style Index approach).

The results are found in Table 5. While the overall return is the same as the Style Index return, the results for individual years have changed. With this variation, most of the bullish market years have lower returns. That's because the system often rotated to the bond fund just as stocks hit their low points after normal market pullbacks. Returns during the equity bear market were improved, however, because bonds did well while stocks were falling.

For details on every transaction and updated performance statistics, visit www.ETFtradingstrategies.com. Past performance does not guarantee future results. For other important assumptions, see Part III Conclusion.

Year	Basic Rotation (%)	S&P 500 Index (%)
1998	44.25	26.67
1999	57.41	19.53
2000	5.34	-10.14
2001	3.35	-13.04
2002	-12.91	-23.37
2003	34.81	26.38
2004	10.65	8.99
2005	-0.74	3.00
2006 *	8.97	3.73
AROI	15.14	3.56

Table 5 - Variation #2 – Adding a Bond Fund
7 ½ round trip trades per year. Average holding period of 96 days.
Through March 31, 2006

Summary

The early 2000s were outstanding years for bond funds. Given this, one would have expected a higher return by adding a bond fund choice. If the overall return didn't increase by adding a bond fund during this time period, then it won't likely increase returns as we move forward.

Still, investors who want to reduce drawdowns may choose to use this variation. During extended bear markets, having half of your portfolio rotate to bonds can be beneficial.

By adding an additional ETF and making sure our current holdings were in the top four positions of the report, as opposed to the top three, the number of short-term whipsaw trades was reduced. Adding an additional ETF fund to the list in Table 1(page 47) is worth doing, but a bond fund may not be the best choice.

Variation #3 – Adding International Funds

The Style Index strategy rotates to broad market segments, such as large-cap growth or small-cap value. In keeping with this concept, it wouldn't make sense to add specific countries. Adding broad international choices, however, fits the approach. For this variation, we'll take the ETF choices found in Table 1, but we will add two broad-based international funds: iShares Int'l Emerging Markets (EEM) and iShares EAFE Int'l Developed Markets (EFA).

That means our strategy rotates between nine ETF choices, so we want to hold ETFs in the top four positions of the report (remember, we want our holdings to be in the top half of the report). If during a rotation period a current holding falls below the top four positions on the relative strength report, then that holding is switched to the ETF with the highest relative strength.

The testing results are found in Table 6.

Year	Basic Rotation (%)	S&P 500 Index (%)
1998	41.60	26.67
1999	54.92	19.53
2000	5.28	-10.14
2001	1.49	-13.04
2002	-15.26	-23.37
2003	49.40	26.38
2004	14.38	8.99
2005	11.88	3.00
2006 *	11.70	3.73
AROI	19.10	3.56

Table 6 - Variation #3 – Adding International Funds
6 round trip trades per year. Average holding period of 111 days.
*Through March 31, 2006

For details on every transaction and updated performance statistics, visit www.ETFtradingstrategies.com. Past performance does not guarantee future results. For other important assumptions, see Part III Conclusion.

Summary

Adding two international choices greatly improved results with less trading. Plus, with more ETF choices the portfolio holdings had a bit more room to fluctuate on the relative strength report, and the number of whipsaw trades was reduced. Because of the emerging market ETF addition, portfolio volatility was increased under this variation. Still, for most people, adding international ETF choices is a good idea. After performing this research, I've added the two international ETF choices to my managed account program (www. ETFportfolios.net).

Chapter 6

Sector ETF Rotation Using Style Index Model

The Style Index rotation model from the last chapter traded market segments, such as large-cap, small-cap, growth, or value. A more aggressive approach is to trade sector ETFs. Examples of sector ETFs are banking, semiconductors, and health -care. They are less diversified and offer a higher profit potential than the style indexes.

The two ETF families that offer the most sector ETFs are iShares (www.ishares.com) and PowerShares (www.powershares.com). Between these two families, there are over forty sector choices.

Back testing a trading strategy for sector ETFs is even harder than testing the Style Index ETFs. Most of the iShares sector funds began in 2000-01 and the PowerShares sector funds began in 2005. Fortunately, sector mutual funds, such as those from Fidelity Investments, have more history and models can be run on these funds. If a model works on Fidelity sector funds, it should work on sector ETFs as well.

Style Index Model on Sector Funds

To begin our analysis of sector ETFs, we'll first apply the Style Index model from Chapter 4 to sector funds. The Style Index model should work well—otherwise, I would lose confidence in the approach. If the model only works for style index ETFs but doesn't work for sector ETFs, then we've fit the model to the data too closely.

Our first test is on the forty-one sector funds from the Fidelity mutual fund family. As explained in Chapter 4, our trading strategy uses a relative strength calculation that looks at the last 120 trading days (approximately six months) and breaks them into quarters. A percentage return figure is calculated for each quarter. These returns are then averaged, with twice the weight placed on the most recent quarter's worth of data. Please visit www.ETFtradingstrategies.com for a posting of current relative strength numbers.

At the start of the test, the two highest ranked Fidelity sector funds were purchased with equal dollar amounts to establish a fully invested portfolio. Two weeks later, the same relative strength report was run again. If the current holdings were rated in the top half of the report (i.e., in the top twenty), then there were no trades. If a holding fell out of the top half in the relative strength report, it was sold and the highest-rated sector fund was purchased. The portfolio was always fully invested in two sector funds.

In our back test, the buy and sell prices used were the closing prices at the end of the week (i.e., the day the reports were run). In actual trading, trades would occur on the following day. Also, the portfolio was rebalanced at the end of each year to create equal positions in the two holdings.

The Results

The strategy is designed to rotate to the sectors of the market that have the best performance. In this case, the testing results are exceptional (Table 7). Our strategy outperformed each year, including the brutal bear market. The 40% return in 2000 is especially

Year	Fidelity Rotation (%)	S&P 500 Index (%)
1998	30.25	26.67
1999	93.77	19.53
2000	39.88	-10.14
2001	-7.65	-13.04
2002	-14.10	-23.37
2003	35.20	26.38
2004	26.35	8.99
2005	25.47	3.00
2006 *	14.96	3.73
AROI	26.30	3.56

Table 7 - Fidelity Sector Fund Returns
3 3/4 round trip trades per year. Average holding period of 200 days.
*Through March 31, 2006

impressive. It shows that the strategy benefited from the technology run at the start of 2000 but by design, it rotated out of technology before the year was finished. From January 1998 through March 2006, the average annual rate of return on the strategy was 26.30%.

Looking at the yearly returns, this is obviously a very aggressive system. Only two funds were held at one time, and there were times when both funds were technology or telecommunications oriented. The portfolio is anything but diversified and is too aggressive for most people. Nevertheless, it shows our trading model works for a variety of investment securities. The model is sound.

For details on every transaction and updated performance statistics, visit www.ETFtradingstrategies.com. Past performance does not guarantee future results. For other important assumptions, see Part III Conclusion.

Testing on Sector ETFs

Our Style Index model works for Fidelity sector funds. How does it work on ETFs? As stated earlier, iShares ETFs began trading in 2001 so our back test starts in 2002. In additional to traditional sectors, we also included four international region ETFs. Most of these ETFs began in 2002 so they are included in our back test beginning in 2003. The list of our sector ETF choices is found in Table 8.

Ticker	ETF
ICF	iShares Realty Majors
IYM	iShares Basic Materials
IYC	iShares Consumer Services
IYK	iShares Consumer Goods
IYE	iShares Energy
IYF	iShares Financial
IYG	iShares Financial Services
IYH	iShares Healthcare
IYJ	iShares Industrial
IYR	iShares Real Estate
IYW	iShares Technology
IYZ	iShares Telecommunications
IDU	iShares Utilities
IGE	iShares Natural Resources
IGN	iShares Networking
IGW	iShares Semiconductors
IGV	iShares Software
IGM	iShares Technology

IBB	iShares Biotechnology
EZU	iShares EMU
IEV	iShares Europe 350
EPP	iShares Pacific Ex-Japan
ITF	iShares Topix 150
ILF	iShares Latin America

Table 8 - Sector ETF Choices
A list of the ETFs used in our sector back test.

The same strategy that was used on the Fidelity sector funds is used on the ETFs in Table 8. In 2002, there were ninteen ETF choices so the portfolio holdings must remain in the top nine places on the relative strength report, or else they are sold (remember, the current holdings need to be in the top half of the report). After 2002, the international funds were added, so the current holdings needed to be in the top twelve places.

The buy and sell prices used were the closing prices at the end of the week (i.e., the day the reports were run). In actual trading, trades would occur on the next day's opening price. A $17 commission was factored in. Also, the portfolio was rebalanced at the end of each year to create equal positions in the two holdings. Dividends were not factored in.

The results are found in Table 9. With the reduced diversification, the yearly returns varied greatly from the market's returns. In the 2005 flat market, the sector portfolio gained 36% because of Energy and Natural Resources holdings. The year 2003 was huge because Networking doubled in value and a Semiconductor holding leaped 27%.

Year	iShares Rotation (%)	S&P 500 Index (%)
2002	-25.43	-23.37
2003	82.73	26.38
2004	6.26	8.99
2005	35.74	3.00
2006 *	10.94	3.73
AROI	20.04	2.87

Table 9 - iShares Sector Fund Returns
5 round trip trades per year. Average holding period of 131 days.
Through March 31, 2006

For details on every transaction and updated performance statistics, visit www.ETFtradingstrategies.com. Past performance does not guarantee future results. For other important assumptions, see Part III Conclusion.

Summary

It is comforting to see that the model that tested well on Style Index ETFs also performed well on Fidelity sector funds and sector ETFs. It is because of its simplicity that it works across different investment vehicles. As long as there is a segment of the market that outperforms, this model will do well. The longer the segment outperforms, the better the system does.

This Sector Rotation model is very aggressive, but there are ways to lower risk. For example, you could hold more than two ETFs and make sure the ETF holdings don't overlap (i.e., you wouldn't hold both Technology and Semiconductors).

Chapter 7

Sector ETF Rotation Research

The Sector Rotation strategy using the Style Index model works well, but can it be improved? Our strategy rotates to the best performing sectors. But should the best performing sectors be measured by computing their one-month performance, six-month performance, or one-year performance? Sectors move faster so maybe the price change report should use a shorter look-back period. That way, you get in sooner and get out earlier. That is what we thought. Testing, however, proved otherwise.

We ran a simple back test on the Fidelity sector funds going back to 1995. Every twenty-two business days (approximately one month), we ran a percentage price change report on the sector funds covering time periods that ranged from one month to one and a half years. The two best performing sector funds were bought and held for twenty-two days. The process was repeated.

The results are found in Table 10. If you looked at how each sector fund performed over the most recent month and then constantly rotated to the two best performers, you would have made approximately 9.86% annually. Results improve when you lengthen the look-back period.

Look-Back Period	Annual % Return
1 Month	9.86
3 Months	15.90
6 Months	16.81
1 Year	19.79
1 ½ Year	15.66

Table 10 - Annual % Return on Fidelity Sector Funds with different Look-Back Periods. *Rotating every 22-days to the best one-year performing sector funds was the best strategy.*

If you rotate to the best six-month performing sector funds, then your return increases to 15.9%. Results further improve until the look-back period reaches one year. After that, the results begin to deteriorate. Rotating to the best one-year performing sector funds worked best.

Are those results consistent with testing on ETFs? Sector ETFs are so new that we can only test back to 2002, but it reveals the same conclusion. Using the twenty-four sector and international ETFs found in Table 8, we rotated to the best performing ETFs using different look-back periods. Once again, we rotated to the best performers every twenty-two days.

The results are found in Table 11. Once again, we found that the best strategy was to buy the ETFs that were the best performers over the prior year.

Look-Back Period	Annual % Return
1 Month	7.47
3 Months	8.39
6 Months	13.97
1 Year	23.21
1 ½ Year	15.10

Table 11 - Return on iShares ETFs with different look-back periods (2002 to May 2006). *Rotating every 22-days to the best one-year performing sector funds was the best strategy.*

Summary

Our ETF trading strategies rotate to the best performing ETFs. Since sector ETFs move faster than more diversified indexes, one would have thought that rotating to the ETFs that recently performed well would improve the results. Not so fast. Rather than buying the best one-month performing ETFs, results were improved by purchasing the best one-year performing ETFs. Catching longer-term trends was more profitable than trying to catch short-term cycles.

We've all heard it before—buying last year's winning mutual fund is a losing strategy. That may be the case if you buy-and-hold the mutual fund. That was not what we were doing. In our test, we bought the best one-year performers but rotated to these best performers every twenty-two business days.

Chapter 8

Sector ETF Trading Model

L et's use what we learned in Chapter 7 to test our Sector Rotation model. Here is how it works. At the start of every month, we calculate a one-year return for the iShares sector and international ETFs in Table 8. The two best performing ETFs are purchased with equal dollar amounts to create a fully invested portfolio. These two ETFs are held for the remainder of the month.

At the start of the following month, the one-year ETF returns are computed again. As long as the current holdings remain the top two performers, then there are no trades. If a holding is no longer one of the two best performers, then it is sold and replaced by the best performing ETF. We do not double into an existing position. This process is repeated at the start of every month.

Let's clarify this with an example. Figure 19 ranks the one-year performance on the first trading day in April 2006. The two best performers, iShares Latin America (ILF) and iShares Networking (IGN), are purchased and held for the remainder of the month.

At the start of May, the one-year ETF returns are ranked again (Figure 20). Latin America remains one of the two best performers so it remains a holding. Networking, however, fell to the fifth

FIGURE 19 - AIQ REPORTS

Reports View Generate Help

AIQ AIQ Reports
├ Stock Reports
│ ├ Expert Analysis
│ ├ Action List
│ ├ Weighted Action List
│ ├ Signal Review
│ ├ New Highs / New Lows
│ ├ Price Change - Upside
│ │ ├ Short Term
│ │ └ **Long Term**
│ ├ Price Change - Downside
│ │ ├ Short Term
│ │ └ Long Term
│ ├ Price Gap
│ ├ Relative Strength - Strong
│ ├ Relative Strength - Weak
│ ├ Volatility Analysis
│ ├ Accumulation / Distribution
│ ├ Persistence of Money Flow
│ ├ Price Volume Divergence
│ ├ Volume Change
│ ├ Volume Spike
│ ├ Volume Trend
│ ├ Mov Avg Crossover - Upsi
│ ├ Mov Avg Crossover - Dow
│ ├ Crossover of Two Mov Av
│ ├ Mov Avg Status - Upside
│ ├ Mov Avg Status - Downsic
│ └ Point & Figure Breakout
├ Group Reports
├ Sector Reports
├ Mutual Fund Reports

Upside Price Change Report
04/03/06 – Daily
Long Term

Ticker	Stock	Percent	Price
ILF	iShares Latin America	81	143.73
IGN	iShares Networking	52	36.78
ITF	iShares Topix 150	48	127.22
IGE	iShares Natural Resources	39	96.67
IGW	iShares Semiconductor	38	65.65
ICF	iShares Realty Majors	32	84.05
IYE	iShares Energy	31	92.68
IBB	iShares Biotechnology	27	81.25
IYR	iShares Real Estate	26	71.90
EZU	iShares EMU	25	87.85
IGM	iShares Technology	24	49.61
IYW	iShares Technology	24	52.46
IEV	iShares Europe 350	21	89.50
EPP	iShares Pacific Ex-Japan	21	106.80
IYJ	iShares Industrial	21	63.33
IYM	iShares Basic Materials	20	56.37
IYF	iShares Financial	19	104.84
IYG	iShares Financial Services	17	119.19
IYZ	iShares Telecommunications	16	25.93
IGV	iShares Software	15	41.61
IYC	iShares Consumer Cyclical	11	61.64
IYH	iShares Healthcare	7	63.46
IYK	iShares Noncyclical	6	53.94
IDU	iShares Utilities	6	75.84

For Help, press F1   NUM

The report was run on list of ETFs and shows ILF and IGN in the top two positions.

position. Networking is sold and iShares Natural Resources (IGE) is purchased.

Table 12 shows the yearly results using this strategy. It is comforting to see that the strategy outperformed in 2002. Profitable trades in real estate helped offset some of the market losses. In early 2005, the portfolio did very well in the face of a mostly flat S&P 500 because of a holding in Latin America.

FIGURE 20 - AIQ REPORTS

```
Reports   View   Generate   Help
[toolbar icons]

AIQ AIQ Reports                          Upside Price Change Report
├ Stock Reports                          05/01/06 — Daily
│ ├ Expert Analysis                      Long Term
│ ├ Action List
│ ├ Weighted Action List      Ticker    Stock                          Percent   Price
│ ├ Signal Review             ILF       iShares Latin America              84    152.73
│ ├ New Highs / New Lows      IGE       iShares Natural Resources          54    103.61
│ ├ Price Change - Upside     ITF       iShares Topix 150                  50    129.54
│ │ ├ Short Term              IYE       iShares Energy                     44     98.22
│ │ ├ Long Term               IGN       iShares Networking                 32     34.68
│ ├ Price Change - Downside   EZU       iShares EMU                        29     90.75
│ │ ├ Short Term              EPP       iShares Pacific Ex-Japan           29    114.35
│ │ ├ Long Term               IYM       iShares Basic Materials            28     59.50
│ ├ Price Gap                 IGW       iShares Semiconductor              28     66.10
│ ├ Relative Strength - Strong IEV      iShares Europe 350                 26     93.06
│ ├ Relative Strength - Weak  ICF       iShares Realty Majors              20     81.44
│ ├ Volatility Analysis       IYJ       iShares Industrial                 19     64.40
│ ├ Accumulation / Distribution IYF     iShares Financial                  16    107.09
│ ├ Persistence of Money Flow IYG       iShares Financial Services         16    122.45
│ ├ Price Volume Divergence   IYR       iShares Real Estate                15     70.00
│ ├ Volume Change             IBB       iShares Biotechnology              15     76.66
│ ├ Volume Spike              IGM       iShares Technology                 15     48.73
│ ├ Volume Trend              IYW       iShares Technology                 14     51.51
│ ├ Mov Avg Crossover - Upsi  IYZ       iShares Telecommunications         13     25.59
│ ├ Mov Avg Crossover - Dow   IGV       iShares Software                    9     41.85
│ ├ Crossover of Two Mov Av   IYC       iShares Consumer Cyclical           7     61.58
│ ├ Mov Avg Status - Upside   IDU       iShares Utilities                   5     76.22
│ ├ Mov Avg Status - Downsic  IYK       iShares Noncyclical                 3     54.18
│ ├ Point & Figure Breakout
├ Group Reports
├ Sector Reports

For Help, press F1                                               NUM
```

A 240-day Price Change report on May 1, 2006. IGN fell out of the top two positions so it is sold; the funds were transferred to IGE.

SOURCE: AIQ SYSTEMS

Year	iShares Rotation (%)	S&P 500 Index (%)
2002	-11.09	-23.37
2003	40.57	26.38
2004	6.31	8.99
2005	33.22	3.00
2006 *	11.19	3.73
AROI	17.20	2.87

Table 12 - iShares Sector Fund Returns
8 1/4 round trip trades per year. Average holding period of 78 days.
*Through March 31, 2006

For details on every transaction and updated performance statistics, visit www.ETFtradingstrategies.com. Past performance does not guarantee future results. For other important assumptions, see Part III Conclusion.

Summary

This Sector ETF strategy had very good results and would be perfect for those with busy lifestyles. Although you would only perform an analysis once a month, the strategy's returns would be well above the market.

There are many ways to modify this system to meet your needs. Holding two ETFs is risky, so you could hold more ETFs using this system. Better yet, you can combine this program with the Style Index model outlined in chapter 6. For those who find it hard to evaluate ETFs just once a month, you can apply this strategy every week. To reduce turnover, you could hold an ETF until it falls out of the top four places (as opposed to the top two).

If you choose to modify our trading systems to fit your own personal trading style, our analysis should provide a good foundation and save you a great deal of time.

Part III Conclusion

Back Testing Assumptions

B ack testing historical data is an effective method for determining technical strategy. Research has shown that the market's behavior patterns do not change dramatically over time. By analyzing past performance of benchmark indexes, we were able to develop workable rotation strategies for ETFs, even though they are a relatively new investment vehicle.

However, there were many assumptions to our tests. The back tests assumed the portfolio was always fully invested in two ETFs. In the Style Index testing, many of the ETFs were not yet available to purchase at the beginning date of the back test. When the ETF wasn't available, the back test used the ETF's benchmark index as a substitute. The back test used price data from the actual ETFs once they became available. Studies show a high, but not exact, correlation between the benchmark indexes and the ETFs.

The percentage returns represent a hypothetical back test, instead of actual performance. The back test's returns and other figures have not been audited but are based upon information obtained from public sources believed to be reliable. Since no funds were managed using the strategies during this period, the impact that economic and market factors might have had on the trading cannot be represented.

The strategies were managed with a view toward capital appreciation with risk levels greater than the S&P 500. Because of turnover rates, portfolios were subject to higher tax costs than portfolios with lesser turnover.

As with any strategy, past performance does not guarantee future results or that losses will not occur.

Part IV

TRADING PSYCHOLOGY

Having an effective trading strategy is essential, but it doesn't guarantee success. The strategy must fit your trading style, and you must have the discipline to follow it. Trading psychology is often an overlooked component in successful trading.

In this section is an important article that was written by Dr. J.D. Smith, the founder of AIQ Systems. Dr. Smith developed AIQ's TradingExpert software to improve his trading. He was a mathematician and scientist who focused on developing unique trading tools. Over time he learned, however, that a trader's success wasn't necessarily defined by the formulas he used. Instead, it was defined by his mental approach. This was quite a finding from a numbers person.

Dr. Smith developed an acronym to help his trading. To be successful, you had to follow a DOFPIC approach. If you didn't, then you'd get PICD-OF (i.e., picked-off). What is DOFPIC? Read on.

Chapter 9

Dr. J.D. Smith Offers a Personal Trading Process

Dr. J.D. Smith

The seminars we present are an excellent opportunity for me to meet and talk with many successful AIQ TradingExpert users. During the last two years, the experience has been extremely valuable to me because of the ideas for new features and systems that come from our users.

The seminars are also valuable to me because I see numerous examples of exactly how top traders use our systems on a daily basis. That exposure plus the recent rash of speeches, articles, and books published on trading discipline, the psychology of trading, and profiles of market wizards has caused me to explore the human side of trading.

What is it about our best users that allow them to be successful traders month after month, year after year? The answer is not how they use our systems, because there are almost as many ways of using them as there are successful traders. The answer lies in personal trading habits.

I have found that the successful trader has a detailed personal trading process that is executed in exactly the same way all the time. That is the answer, a personal trading process that never varies. Without such a trading process, the chance of consistent success is severely reduced. The question now becomes—how does one develop a trading process?

Developing a trading process can be an interesting challenge because, to be useful, it must be personal. Each of us must develop one in our own way. This is important because in order for our trading process to be effective, it must match our personality; it must take advantage of our strengths, and it must compensate for our weaknesses. We must believe in it, and believe what it will do for us. We must own our own process.

A trading process is a detailed, step-by-step implementation of our personal trading plan. Thankfully, there exists a body of knowledge to assist in developing such a plan.

The general theory of command systems offers useful concepts of planning and control. The literature on trading techniques and trading discipline offers numerous personal qualities that have an impact on trading success. Combining planning and control concepts with the qualities of good trading practice provides us with a suitable framework upon which to build our own trading process.

None of these personal qualities are particularly new. They are heavily discussed in the literature on personal behavior as well as trading. None of the planning concepts are new. They have been developed over many years of study of command and control theory. What is new is the handle I have given to this combined approach. I call it DOFPIC, which stands for the qualities necessary for successful trading: discipline, organization, focus, patience, independence, and confidence.

We must develop the discipline to organize and focus our trading activities into an intelligent process. With discipline comes the patience, independence, and confidence essential to successful trading. In a word, DOFPIC. I find it much easier to just say (to myself, of course) that I am a DOFPIC kind of guy. However you may do it, I find it beneficial to use DOFPIC as a personal "mantra," and I suggest repeating it often as positive self-talk.

The design of a trading process is critical to the development and nurturing of the DOFPIC qualities. As we approach this objective, it is useful to remember the principles used for designing command and control systems:

Principle One—Goal Orientation

Understand the goals of the process and constantly review those goals to ensure their applicability over time.

Principle Two—Transformation

Understand the transformations from market information to decisions to action, a rule inherent in any trading process.

Principle Three—Control

Recognize the need for control over the execution of the process and the outcome of the process, the return.

Principle Four—Periodic Evaluation and Review

Modify the trading process to reflect changes over time in environment, information, technology, the trader, and the market itself.

The qualities represented by DOFPIC transcend trading the stock market, but they have special significance here because adroit application of these qualities will allow us to meet some of our personal objectives.

D   *Discipline* is the ability to follow our trading plan, which allows us to control the fear and greed that are the prime motivations moving the market.

O   *Organization* is the specific process—the daily logs, the money management rules, and the risk management stops we use to execute the plan.

F   *Focus* is the quality that allows us to be specific on which market instruments we trade and our role in the trading process.

P   *Patience* is a constant reminder to trade carefully and to wait until our market has a shape that offers a very good chance of success.

I   *Independence* is the ability to ignore advice and tips from people outside of the AIQ world, people who most certainly know less about what is going on than we do.

C   *Confidence* is our assurance in ourselves and in our trading process. It follows from the other qualities and is absolutely required for successful trading.

There is no one starting point. It is just as meaningful to start, for example, with confidence and to ask what qualities are needed to be a confident trader. Not surprising, the answer is independence, patience, focus, organization, discipline, and an intelligent trading process.

In the final analysis, it is up to each one of us to design our own personal trading process that we believe in and trust. A trading process that matches our personality, takes advantage of our strengths, and compensates for our weaknesses. In the end, this process will help us reach our personal objectives.

Appendix I

RECOMMENDED READING

Chapter 1

Gastineau, Gary. 2002. *The Exchange-Traded Funds Manual.*
New York: John Wiley & Sons, Inc.

Chapter 2

Brooks, John. 2005. *Mastering Technical Analysis.* McGraw-Hill.

Edwards, Robert D., and Magee, John. 2001. *Technical Analysis of
Stock Trends.* American Management Association.

For more educational information from Linda Bradford Raschke,
visit www.ETFtradingstrategies.com.

Chapter 3

Bulkowski, Thomas N. 2005. *Encyclopedia of Chart Patterns.*
New York: John Wiley & Sons, Inc.

For more articles from Steve Palmquist,
visit www.ETFtradingstrategies.com

Chapter 5

Siegel, Jeremy J. 2005. *The Future For Investors.* Crown Business.

Journal of Indexes – www.indexuniverse.com/joi

Chapter 7

Krapivin, Yuri, Yuk Ping Ng, Pierre Oustinow, Jonathan Stein-
metz, and Terence Tong. "Use of Momentum in
Trading Across Industry Sectors." Duke University.
http://www.charttricks.com/Resources/Articles/use of
momentum.pdf

Chapter 10

Douglas, Mark. 1990. *The Disciplined Trader: Developing Winning Attitudes.* New York Institute of Finance.

Appendix II

SOURCES

Swisher, Peter. "Solving an Employer's Fiduciary Dilemma: Liability, Discretion, and the Role of the Qualified Plan Advisor." *Journal of Financial Planning* (February 2004), http://www.fpanet.org/journal/articles/2004_Issues/jfp0204.cfm

Chubb Specialty Insurance. "Fiduciary Liability Loss Prevention." http://www.chubb.com/businesses/csi/chubb4035.html

Elswick, Jill. July 2003. "Scandals Spur Fiduciary Liability Premiums." *Employee Benefits News.*

Elswick, Jill. December 2004. "Caution Advised on Company Stock in Plans." *Employee Benefits News.*

Saxon, Steve, Groom Law Group. November 2005. "Tips on Securing Fiduciary Liability Insurance." www.PlanSponsor.com.

Larsen, Mark, Tillinghast-Towers Perrin. July 2001. "Fiduciary Liabilities Basics." http://www.irmi.com/Expert/Articles/2001/Larsen07.aspx

Reish, Fred. February 2005. "Taking Stock: The Most Dangerous Investment." http://www.reish.com/publications/article_detail.cfm?ARTICLEID=505

Reish, Fred. June 2003. "Taking Stock: Managing the Risk of Company Stock." http://www.reish.com/publications/article_detail.cfm?ARTICLEID=382

AON. March 2005. "Fiduciary & Investment Issues: Beyond the Basics." http://www.aon.com/about/publications/research_briefs/fiduciary_investment.jsp

Gordon, Catherine D. June 2004. "Investment Committees: Vanguard's View of Best Practices." http://www.vanguard.com/pdf/ICRIC_062004.pdf

Greycourt. 2003. "White Paper No. 31—Reinvigorating the Investment Committee." http://www.greycourt.com/whitepapers/WhitePaper031.pdf

Free 2 Week Trial Offer for U.S. Residents From Investor's Business Daily:

INVESTOR'S BUSINESS DAILY will provide you with the facts, figures, and objective news analysis you need to succeed.

Investor's Business Daily is formatted for a quick and concise read to help you make informed and profitable decisions.

This book, along with other books, is available at discounts that make it realistic to provide it as a gift to your customers, clients, and staff. For more information on these long lasting, cost effective premiums, please call us at (800) 272-2855 or you may email us at sales@traderslibrary.com.

$19.95 US

"Finally ... a comprehensive book on Exchange Traded Funds! I have always enjoyed reading David Vomund's insights on the markets and his interviews with other successful traders, and I know you will prosper from the wealth of information contained in this ground-breaking book."

Price Headley, *CFA, CMT*
Founder, BigTrends.com

Want to know how to trade the hottest new investment vehicle?

This book reveals the secrets of profiting from a new and growing investment vehicle—the Exchange Traded Fund. Pulling from experts in the field like Linda Bradford Raschke and Steve Palmquist, this book has all the information you need to begin trading ETFs for profit:

- Learn the basics of ETFs; how they work, why they're growing in popularity, and how you can get your share of the profits.
- Discover the way to apply classic techniques to leverage your ETF investments for both the short-term and long-term.
- Study simple but highly effective mechanical ETF rotation techniques (style, sector, and international) that are now available to the individual investor.

ETF Trading Strategies Revealed doesn't end there. Learn from long-time trader and founder of AIQ Systems, Dr. J.D. Smith, what it takes to mentally be the best. When you have the emotional discipline to follow his techniques, you'll find increased profits aren't far behind.

MARKETPLACE BOOKS®
9002 RED BRANCH ROAD
COLUMBIA MD 21045

ISBN 1-59280-258-3